ELVA M

lifeboat w

Lifeboat Theatre
in association with
widsith
present

S-27
by Sarah Grochala

finboroughtheatre

First performance at the Finborough Theatre, London:
Tuesday, 9 June 2009

S-27

by Sarah Grochala

Cast in order of appearance

May **Pippa Nixon**

Boy **Kate Ward**

Man **Jack Pierce**

June **Brooke Kinsella**

Mother **Amelia Saberwal**

Girl **Kate Ward**

Cousin **Amelia Saberwal**

Col **Tom Reed**

A room in a building that used to be a school.

The performance lasts approximately eighty minutes.

There is no interval.

Director **Stephen Keyworth**

Designer **Olivia Altaras**

Lighting Designer **Gary Bowman**

Production Electrician **Chris Gunnell**

Assistant Director **Eleanor Rhode**

Casting **Rionnach McDaid-Wren**

Press **Jenny Eldridge at Target-Live**

Cover Image **Iona Firouzabadi**

Produced by **Sarah Hudson**

Presented by **Lifeboat** in association with **widsith**

Our patrons are respectfully reminded that, in this intimate theatre, any noise such as rustling programmes, talking or the ringing of mobile phones may distract the actors and your fellow audience-members.

BROOKE KINSELLA
JUNE

Theatre includes *Torn* (Arcola Theatre), *Time of My Life* (Theatre Royal, Northampton), *School Play* (Soho Theatre), and *I Was Jimmy Lennon*.

Television includes *Vital Signs*, *Rose and Maloney*, *Jericho*, *EastEnders*, *The Vice*, *The Bill*, *Just Like Dad*, *Killer*, *Kid in the Corner*, *Sunburn*, *Hope and Glory*, *Rocket to the Moon*, *Maisie Raine*, *Coming Home* and *No Child of Mine*.

Film includes *The Feral Generation*, *Just Like Dad* and *Kevin*.

PIPPA NIXON MAY

Trained at Manchester Metropolitan University. She received an Ian Charleson Award commendation in 2007 for her performance in *The Merchant of Venice*.

Theatre includes *A Midsummer Night's Dream*, *Timon of Athens*, *The Merchant of Venice* (Shakespeare's Globe), *Days of Significance* (Royal Shakespeare Company at the Tricycle Theatre), *Joe Guy* (Soho Theatre), *The Trestle at Pope Lick Creek* (Belfast and Tour), *Project D: I'm Mediocre* (BAC and Tristan Bates Theatre), *The Method* (Oval House Theatre) and *Balm in Gilead* (Young Vic).

Television includes *Wannabes*, *Dream Team*, *Holby City*, *The Bill* and *24Seven*.

JACK PIERCE MAN

Trained at Drama Centre.

Theatre includes *A Streetcar Named Desire*, *Frozen*, *The Power Book* (National Theatre), *Sparkleshark* (National Theatre Tour), and *Biloxi Blues*, *Othello* (National Youth Theatre).

Television includes *Doctors*, *True Heroes – Hostage*, *Silent Witness*, *Blitz*, *Eleventh Hour*, *Footballers Wives*, *Extra Time*, *Holby City*, *EastEnders*, *Ultimate Force*, *Murphy's Law*, *Strange*, *Back Home*, *London's Burning*, *Coupling*, *Black Books*, *Dance*, *Forgive and Forget*, *Babes in the Wood*, *The Bill* and *The Jump*.

Film includes *Clubbed*, *Dummy*, *Shooting Dogs*, *Alien vs Predator*, *Revenge*, *Birthday Girl*, *Gangster No.1* and *The Escort*.

TOM REED COL

Trained at The Arts Educational School of Acting and was nominated for the 2007 Spotlight Award.

Theatre whilst training includes *Gormenghast*, *Radium Girls*, *As You Like It*, *Measure For Measure*, *The Three Sisters* and *Someone Who'll Watch Over Me*.

Film includes *Shadows In The Sun* and *Life Goes On*.

AMELIA SABERWAL
MOTHER / COUSIN

Amelia trained at Webber Douglas Academy of Dramatic Art.

Theatre includes *Thoughtless* (BAFTA), *Silent Cry* (Lyric Hammersmith and National Tour), *Feelgood* (Vienna and Frankfurt English Theatres), *Landscapes After Exile* (Lyric Hammersmith), *Shah Mat* (Reading), *A Waiting Room For Journeying Souls* (Peepul Centre, Leicester), *Feelgood* (Rosemary Branch), *Dawning Of Eve* (Exeter).

Film includes *WMD* (Cannes 2008) and *Fused* (BAFTA 2008).

Television includes *Hustle V* and *The Bill*.

KATE WARD
BOY / GIRL

Trained at the Central School of Speech and Drama.

Theatre whilst training includes *The Wedding Party*, *The Bold and Bright Design*, *Absolute Hell*, *Cuts*,

King Lear, The Innocent Mistress, The Crucible, A Midsummer Night's Dream, and The Last Ones.

Theatre includes An Ideal Husband (Royal Exchange Theatre, Manchester). Film includes The Last Jazz Musician.

SARAH GROCHALA PLAYWRIGHT

S-27 won the inaugural iceandfire/Amnesty International Protect the Human Playwriting Competition and was also shortlisted for the King's Cross Award 2007. Sarah is a graduate of the MPhil in Playwriting Studies at Birmingham University and was recently commissioned to write a short play to celebrate the twentieth anniversary of the course. Other theatre includes Viable Alternatives (Theatre 503), Gift (King's Head), Waiting for Romeo (Pleasance London and Edinburgh Festival) and Open Ground (Theatro Technis). Radio includes Covent Garden (Theatre Voice and Theatre 503). Sarah originally trained as an actress at Drama Centre. Theatre includes the lead role in Little Women (Duchess Theatre) and Thea Sharrock's Top Girls (BAC). Television includes Judge John Deed, Every Woman Knows a Secret and Storm Damage.

STEPHEN KEYWORTH DIRECTOR

At the Finborough Theatre, Stephen wrote Dog Well Done (2000) – which won the Amnesty International Freedom Of Expression Theatre Award – and directed Fanny and Faggot by Jack Thorne (2007) which transferred to the Pleasance, Edinburgh and London's Trafalgar Studios. He studied Drama at Manchester University. He is Artistic Director of 5065 Lift, a new writing company who produce new work for unusual locations including a two metre square portable elevator, and who took over the London Eye for a one-night arts festival in 2005. Directing includes The Traducers, Dinner With Bono (Flight 5065 on the London Eye), The Powder Jars, Honolulu, Aliens Are Scary (Pleasance, Edinburgh, and 5065 Lift),

BBC Comedy's The Last Laugh Sitcom Competition Final (Ealing Studios), The Amazing Adventures of Schroedinger's Cat, George Orwell's 1984 School Disco, The Service Elevator (Soho Theatre and 5065 Lift), Eyes and Teeth (National Tour), Pravda, Who's Afraid Of Virginia Woolf? (The Green Room, Manchester).

Writing for theatre includes Dead Heat (YMT:UK), A (Gay Disabled Transexual) Love Story Told To A Ticket Inspector At Alton Towers (Theatre Workshop, Edinburgh), Zimbabwe Boy (National Theatre and Flight 5065), Second Revolution (West Yorkshire Playhouse), Mad For It which was nominated for Best New Play at the Manchester Evening News Theatre Awards (Royal Exchange Theatre, Manchester), Clean Sheets and Bloody Games (Royal Court Young Writers), and Fear Of Water (Orange Tree Theatre, Richmond, and Contact Theatre Young Writer's Festival).

Stephen was one of eight writers on the BBC Writer's Academy 2006. Television writing includes EastEnders, Casualty, and Doctors.

Writing for radio includes Gondwanaland, Love My Rifle More Than You, and My Difficult Second Album (BBC Radio 4).

OLIVIA ALTARAS DESIGNER

At the Finborough Theatre, Olivia was Assistant Scenic Artist on Sweethearts (2007).

Studied History of Art and English at The University of Leeds. Theatre design includes Rose Bruford Symposium Festival (Punchdrunk), Interludes (London Games Fringe Festival). As Collaborative Designer, Netaudio Festival (Shunt). As part of the Design Team, The Masque of the Red Death (Punchdrunk at BAC). As Set Dresser, The Vagina Monologues (New Players' Theatre). As Assistant Scenic Artist, Carmen, Madame Butterfly (Royal Albert Hall). As Propmaker, Mary Poppins, The Sound of Music, The Lord Mayor's Show (Russell Beck Studio). Film Design includes *Orlena* (London Film School). As Art Department: *The Disappeared* (Lost Tribe Productions). Television work includes Assistant Scenic Artist on *Marie Lloyd* (BBC Four) and *Bill and Ben* (CBBC). Olivia was also Co-Curator on the photographic exhibition – *Reflections: Democratic Kampuchea and Beyond* at Tuol Sleng, Phnom Penh.

GARY BOWMAN
LIGHTING DESIGNER

Gary trained at Bristol Old Vic Theatre School specialising in Lighting Design. He is an Associate Member of the Association of Lighting Designers. Lighting Designs include *Nowhere Man* (Etcetera Theatre), *So Jest End* (New Players Theatre), *Platform and Christopher* (Etcetera Theatre), *Miller* (Pleasance London), *Calculating Mr One* (National Tour), *Angel and the Muse* (Pleasance London), *Johnny Space Hopper* (National Tour), *A Midsummer Night's Dream* (Abbey House Gardens, Malmesbury), and *Jesus Christ Superstar*, *HONK*, *Children of Eden* and *Annie Get Your Gun* (all at Stagedoor Manor, New York). He has also worked in the West End on *Wicked*, *The Lover and The Collection*, *Buddy*, *Dickens Unplugged*, and *Chicago*.

ELEANOR RHODE
ASSISTANT DIRECTOR

Eleanor Rhode is currently a Resident Assistant Director at the Finborough Theatre where she was Assistant Director on *Trying* (2009) and will direct Michael Healey's *Generous* in August 2009. She is also the co-founder and Artistic Director of Glow Worm, a new theatre company devoted to producing short plays. Direction includes *The Error of Their Ways* (Cockpit Theatre), *A Number* (Camden People's Theatre), *This Lime Tree Bower* (performed at seven different venues over seven nights around Edinburgh and revived for the Edinburgh Festival), *Barefoot in the Park* (Edinburgh Festival and *Suspicion*

and *Dogg's Hamlet* (Bedlam Theatre). She was Associate Director on *Lie of the Land* (Arcola Theatre, Pleasance Edinburgh), *African Gothic* (White Bear Theatre) and *Terrorism* (Oval House Theatre).

RIONNACH McDAID-WREN
CASTING

S-27 is Ri's first project as Casting Director. She has assisted Ginny Schiller on projects for Regent's Park Open Air Theatre, The Rose Theatre Kingston, Theatre Royal Bath, Liverpool Playhouse and English Touring Theatre. As Stage Manager, credits include *Waiting for Romeo* (Pleasance Theatre), *Newley: The Fool Who Dared to Dream* (Upstairs at the Gatehouse), and as Assistant Stage Manager *Into the Woods* (Upstairs at the Gatehouse).

SARAH HUDSON   PRODUCER

Theatre includes *I Found My Horn* (Tristan Bates Theatre) and *Waiting for Romeo* (Pleasance London). Film includes *Gooseberries Don't Dance*. Television includes numerous TV adverts, promos and idents.

Acknowledgements

Lifeboat Theatre and widsith would like to thank Matt Delbridge, Timothy Hughes, Host Universal and Queen Mary University of London for their generous help and support.

lifeboat

Lifeboat were formed to develop challenging new writing, to re-invent and re-imagine the relationship between audience and performers and to continue the work started by 5065 Lift.

For three years, 5065 Lift developed new work with writers including Jack Thorne, Joy Wilkinson, Mark Norfolk, Darren Murphy and George Gotts and presented it in unusual locations including Brighton Beach, the corridors and balconies of Soho Theatre and inside a two metre square portable elevator.

"The very confines of this space fuel the imagination... the standard of writing is so very high, I can't recommend it enough." Scotland on Sunday.

Their work culminated in 2005 when Flight 5065 took over the London Eye for one night, filling it with theatre, comedy and music. Of the thirty to forty shows, fourteen were commissioned especially, and unusually the night brought the National Theatre, the Royal Court Theatre, Soho Theatre and Paines Plough together to work in the same space, alongside artists such as Damon Albarn, Beth Orton, Arthur Smith and Jo Brand.

Lifeboat's first production was *Fanny and Faggot* by Jack Thorne, staged in an early version in 2004 in the 5065 Lift, and developed for a sell-out run at the Finborough Theatre in February 2007, before transferring to the Pleasance Edinburgh and Trafalgar Studios in London's West End. *S-27* is their second production.

widsith

Widsith was founded in 2006 by the director Nina Brazier and the playwright Sarah Grochala. The company specialises in working with new writing and nurtures emerging talent by offering playwrights practical support. This includes feedback on scripts, as well as the opportunity to work collaboratively on promising ideas with a dramaturg and a company of actors. The company's first production *Waiting for Romeo* was staged at the Edinburgh Festival in 2006 and was revived at the Pleasance London in January 2009. The company has also produced several rehearsed readings including *After Amber* by James Woolf and *Clancy's Famous Velveteens* by Richard Marsh.

finboroughtheatre

118 Finborough Road,
London SW10 9ED
admin@finboroughtheatre.co.uk
www.finboroughtheatre.co.uk

Artistic Director | Neil McPherson
Resident Designer | Alex Marker
General Manager |
Anna Bartholomew
Pearson Playwright-in-Residence |
Anders Lustgarten
Playwrights-in-Residence |
James Graham, Al Smith,
Alexandra Wood
Literary Associate | Titas Halder
Resident Casting Director |
Rachel Payant
Chief Electrician | Oliver Luff
Master Carpenter | Jessi James
Resident Assistant Directors |
Ellie Browning, Ben Kidd, Tim Newns,
Eleanor Rhode

The Finborough Theatre has support
of the Pearson Playwrights' Scheme.
Sponsored by
Pearson PLC.

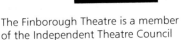

The Finborough Theatre is a member
of the Independent Theatre Council
and Musical Theatre Matters UK

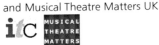

Mailing

Please email us at
admin@finboroughtheatre.co.uk or
give your details to our Box Office
staff to join our free mailing list.
If you would like to be sent a free
season leaflet every three months,
just include your postal address and
postcode.

Feedback

We welcome your comments,
complaints and suggestions. Email
neilmcpherson@
finboroughtheatre.co.uk or write to
Finborough Theatre, 118 Finborough
Road, London SW10 9ED.

Friends

The Finborough Theatre is a
registered charity. We receive no
public funding, and rely solely on the
support of our audiences. Please do
consider supporting us by becoming
a member of our Friends of the
Finborough Theatre scheme. There
are four categories of Friends, each
offering a wide range of benefits.

Richard Tauber Friends –
Charles Lascelles.

Lionel Monckton Friends –
Anonymous. Philip and
Christine Carne.

William Terriss Friends – Tom Erhardt.
Leo and Janet Liebster. Peter Lobl.

finboroughtheatre

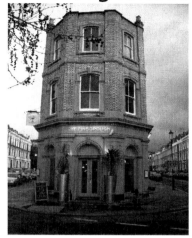

"One of the most stimulating venues in London, fielding a programme that is a bold mix of trenchant, politically thought-provoking new drama and shrewdly chosen revivals of neglected works from the past."
The Independent

"A disproportionately valuable component of the London theatre ecology. Its programme combines new writing and revivals, in selections intelligent and audacious." Financial Times

"A blazing beacon of intelligent endeavour, nurturing new writers while finding and reviving neglected curiosities from home and abroad."
The Daily Telegraph

"Few leading fringe theatres have walked off with so many awards or promoted such a rich variety of writers as the Finborough."
Plays International

"The Finborough Theatre has developed a reputation out of all proportion to its tiny size. It has played its part in the careers of many remarkable playwrights, directors, and actors."
Financial Times

The multi-award-winning Finborough Theatre – led by Artistic Director Neil McPherson – presents both plays and music theatre, concentrated exclusively on new writing and rediscoveries of neglected works from the 19th and 20th centuries. We also run a Resident Assistant Director Programme and a vibrant Literary Department.

Founded in 1980, artists working at the theatre in the 1980s included Clive Barker, Rory Bremner, Nica Burns, Kathy Burke, Ken Campbell and Clare Dowie. In the 1990s, the Finborough Theatre became particularly known for new writing, including Naomi Wallace's first play *The War Boys*; Rachel Weisz in David Farr's *Neville Southall's Washbag*; four plays by Anthony Neilson including *Penetrator* and *The Censor*, both of which transferred to the Royal Court Theatre; and new plays by Tony Marchant, David Eldridge, Mark Ravenhill and Phil Willmott. New writing development included Mark Ravenhill's *Shopping and F***king* (Royal Court, West End and Broadway), Conor McPherson's *This Lime Tree Bower* (Bush Theatre) and Naomi Wallace's *Slaughter City* (Royal Shakespeare Company).

Since 2000, New British plays have included Laura Wade's London debut with her adaptation of W H Davies' *Young Emma*, commissioned for the Finborough Theatre; Simon Vinnicombe's *Year 10* which went on to play at BAC's Time Out Critics' Choice Season; James Graham's *Albert's Boy* with Victor Spinetti; Joy Wilkinson's *Fair* which transferred to the West End; and Nicholas de Jongh's *Plague Over England* which transferred to the West End. London premieres have included Jack Thorne's *Fanny and Faggot* which also transferred to the West End. Many of the Finborough Theatre's new plays have been published and are available to purchase from our website.

UK premieres of foreign plays have included Brad Fraser's *Wolfboy*; Lanford Wilson's *Sympathetic Magic*; Larry Kramer's *The Destiny of Me*; Tennessee Williams' *Something Cloudy, Something Clear*; Frank McGuinness' *Gates of Gold* with William Gaunt and the late John Bennett in his last stage role (which also transferred to the West End); Nilo Cruz's *Hortensia and the Museum of Dreams* with Linda Bassett; the English premiere of Robert McLellan's Scots language classic, *Jamie the Saxt*; and Joe DiPietro's *F***king Men*, currently playing at the King's Head Theatre.

Rediscoveries of neglected work have included the first London revivals of Rolf Hochhuth's *Soldiers* and *The Representative*; both parts of Keith Dewhurst's *Lark Rise to Candleford*; *The Women's War*, an evening of original suffragette plays; *Etta Jenks* with Clarke Peters and Daniela Nardini; *The Gigli Concert* with Niall Buggy and Paul McGann; Noël Coward's first play, *The Rat Trap*; Charles Wood's *Jingo* with Susannah Harker; and the sell-out production of Patrick Hamilton's *Hangover Square*.

Music Theatre has included the new (premieres from the UK and USA by Grant Olding, Charles Miller, Michael John LaChuisa, Adam Guettel, Andrew Lippa and Adam Gwon) and the old (the sell-out Celebrating British Music Theatre series, reviving forgotten British musicals).

The Finborough Theatre was the inaugural winner of the Empty Space Peter Brook Award's Dan Crawford Pub Theatre Award in 2005 which it also won again in 2008, as well as winning the Empty Space Peter Brook Mark Marvin Award in 2004. The Finborough Theatre was the only unfunded theatre to be awarded the prestigious Pearson Playwriting Award bursary for Chris Lee in 2000, Laura Wade in 2005, James Graham in 2006, Al Smith in 2007 and Anders Lustgarten in 2009 – as well as the Pearson Award for Best Play for Laura Wade in 2005 and James Graham in 2007. Neil McPherson was named Best Artistic Director in the 2009 Fringe Report Awards.

www.finboroughtheatre.co.uk

S-27

First published in 2009 by Oberon Books Ltd
521 Caledonian Road, London N7 9RH
Tel: 020 7607 3637 / Fax: 020 7607 3629
e-mail: info@oberonbooks.com
www.oberonbooks.com

A catalogue record for this book is available from the British
Library.

ISBN: 978-1-84002-930-7

Cover photograph by Iona Firouzabadi

Printed in Great Britain by CPI Antony Rowe, Chippenham.

Characters

MAY
JUNE
BOY
MAN
MOTHER
GIRL
COUSIN
COL

For Nay Nân

SCENE ONE

A classroom. A black board hangs on the wall. There are still pieces of chalk by it. The rest of the walls are covered with fading educational posters. In front of the black board is a small raised area on which the teacher's desk sits. There is an exercise book on the desk and a pen. The student's desks and chairs have been stacked to one side. A bookcase full of books. Two doors. A door stage left is the entrance to the room, while a door stage right is the exit from the room. All exits and entrances in the play are through the stage left door. There are windows. The room is illuminated with soft morning light. A chair is positioned in the light. There is a manual camera set up on a tripod. A girl, MAY, is by the camera. She is dressed in a neat and uniform manner. She has no make up on. Everything about her appearance is meticulous. There is not a hair out of place. A BOY is sitting on the chair. His clothes are crumpled and dirty. His head is bowed. A tag which reads S-27 is pinned to his clothes.

MAY: Head up.

> *The BOY does not respond.*

Head up.

> *The BOY still does not respond.*

Look at me. You have to look at me.

> *Pause.*

It's just a photograph. A stupid photograph. Ain't gonna hurt you.

> *The BOY lifts his head.*

There, that's better. That's a good boy. Hold it there.

> *The BOY bursts into tears.*

BOY: I want my mum.

MAY: She's outside.

BOY: I want her.

MAY: You'll see her in a minute.

BOY: I want her now.

MAY: She's waiting for you, waiting for you, in the truck.

BOY: Now. Now.

MAY: If you don't shut up and hold up your head, I'm gonna have to get them in here and they'll hold it up for you. Understand? Do you want that? Do you? Cos they're just outside. I'm gonna count to three. One... Two. . .

The BOY holds his head up.

And wipe them tears off your face.

The BOY tries to wipe his face with his hands.

Here.

MAY gives him her handkerchief. He cleans his face.

Good.

MAY takes the picture. Blackout.

SCENE TWO

The same. The books have been taken off the bookcase and there is now a wooden rack containing number tags on the top shelf. The tags are in order. The first tag at the front of the box reads S-51. There is a space next to it where the rack starting S-1 would be. A MAN now sits in the chair. His showy clothes are threadbare. He wears the S-27 tag. MAY is examining the camera. The MAN sizes her up. She bends over to clean the lens.

MAN: Nice.

Pause.

Good to a see a girl with some meat on her, that's all I'm saying.

Pause.

Come on, cheer up love. Ain't the end of the world…go on give us a smile. You know you wanna.

MAY looks through the lens of the camera

Bet you've got a lovely smile, beautiful girl like you.

She looks at the MAN directly.

What?

Pause.

If you ain't careful, the wind'll change and you'll get stuck all serious like that

MAY gets her notebook.

and then you'll be sorry…

MAY: Name?

MAN: You wanna know my name?

MAY: Yes.

MAN: And why would you wanna know that?

MAY: For your file.

MAN: That's all is it?

MAY: Yes.

MAN: Tell you what…you tell me yours, I'll tell you mine.

MAY: Name.

MAN: Have a guess. Go on.

MAY: I ain't got no time for games.

MAN: I reckon yours is something precious, something delicate. Like Rose?

MAY: Name.

MAN: Or Violet, or Lil…

MAY: Do you want me to get them in here?

MAN: Ow, you don't wanna do that...

MAY: I'll get em. I will. You know what they'll do to you.

MAN: Don't you wanna do it yourself?

MAY: I ain't gonna touch you.

MAN: Really?

MAY: Ain't my job. I ain't permitted.

MAN: What's the matter?

MAY: Name.

MAN: You know you wanna...

MAY: Now.

MAN: Come on. Don't you like it?

MAY: Tell me your fucking name.

JUNE enters. She is a year or two younger than MAY. She is dressed in identical clothes but her appearance lacks MAY's close attention to detail. She is holding a bowl of food.

What?

JUNE: Second bell's gone. Didn't want you to miss it.

MAY: Thanks.

JUNE puts the bowl of food down.

JUNE: It's no bother. Been taking ages this one.

MAY: Camera got jammed.

JUNE: D'you need any help?

MAY: I fixed it.

JUNE: He was being a right pain outside. Mr Chief of Police. Do you want me to erm...

MAY: Ain't no need.

JUNE: Ain't no trouble…

MAY: It's fine.

JUNE: Sure?

MAY: Sure. Thanks erm…?

JUNE: June.

MAY: June.

JUNE exits.

MAN: All right is it? The food here?

MAY: It's okay.

MAN: Smells good.

MAY: What district?

MAN: What?

MAY: What district were you Chief of Police?

MAN: You gonna eat that are you?

MAY: In a minute.

MAN: Right.

MAY: You gonna answer the question?

MAN: What does it matter?

MAY: I'm interested.

MAN: Are you now?

Pause.

MAY: Hungry?

MAN: Just a bit peckish, you know how it is.

MAY: Fancy some lunch?

MAN: That'd be nice, yeah.

MAY: What district?

MAN: Just up in the North country.

MAY: Where?

MAN: Nowhere much. Right in the marshland. Nothing but peasants and chickens.

Silence.

So?

MAY: What?

MAN: The food?

MAY: You want the food?

MAN: You did say?

MAY: Yeah, I did, didn't I?

She gets the bowl.

Here.

She offers it to him.

MAN: Thanks.

He reaches for it. She pulls it away.

MAY: Go on.

MAY offers the bowl again. The man reaches for it. MAY pulls it away.

MAN: Very funny.

MAY offers the bowl again. Pause.

MAY: Ain't you hungry?

The man lunges for the bowl and nearly gets it. MAY smashes the bowl on the floor. Silence.

MAN: You fucking bitch. Do you know what you've done? Do you know what you just did? It's all right for you lot, you lot all cushy up here. You ain't been working twelve hours a day, in the fucking fields, in the hot sun. With nothing but a handful of rice and a bowl of that fucking filthy water you call soup. Famished, that's what I am, fucking starving, and / you just…

MAY: You don't know what hunger is.

MAN: Don't I?

MAY: You'd be down there on your knees if you did.

Pause.

You don't remember do you?

MAN: What?

MAY: I knew I knew you.

MAN: I doubt it.

MAY: It was ages ago. When you was Chief of Police. We had a cow.

MAN: A cow?

MAY: My dad worked his hands off to get that cow.

MAN: So?

MAY: Then you turn up, you and your mates, in your big jeep.

MAN: Ain't got nothing to do with me.

The MAN slowly crouches down and starts to shovel the food off the floor and into his mouth.

MAY: I slip under the house like I was always told and I see dad racing to get the cow in.

MAY gets the tripod and repositions the camera.

But it's too late… You've seen him.

21

MAN: Me?

MAY: You head straight for him. On the wind I can hear his voice, all high and fast like a girl's. He clutches at you. He drops to his knees. But it's no good. You get out a knife.

MAN: What?

MAY: You get out a knife. The cow shrieks and it stumbles.

MAY tries to take the MAN's picture. The MAN prevents her from getting a clean shot.

And then you drag it away still twitching and bleeding, drag it away through the mud.

MAN: He could have said no.

MAY: Could he?

MAN: If he'd had the guts.

MAY: Or wanted to lose his toes.

MAN: What?

MAY: That's what you did to the man next door.

MAN: You've made a mistake.

MAY: No, I ain't. Yours ain't a face I'm gonna forget. Everything we had went into getting that cow. We went through hell that winter. Broke my father it did, broke him in two.

The MAN looks directly at MAY.

MAN: Where is he now?

Pause.

What happened to your family?

MAY: There is no family.

MAN: Of course.

MAY: The Organisation's my family.

MAN: What did they do to them?

MAY: Plenty left. Ain't you gonna lick it clean?

MAN: Think it's funny? This? Do you?

Pause.

Just you wait, just you wait…because it won't be long until I'm back where I belong and you're the one down on the ground grovelling for mercy.

MAY takes the MAN's picture.

MAY: You finished?

MAN: Just you wait…

MAY: That door.

The MAN gets up. He hesitates.

That door.

MAN: And then what?

Blackout.

SCENE THREE

The same. The student's desks and chairs have been removed. There are more racks of tags on the bookcase. A woman is standing in the room. Her stylish dress is filthy and tattered. She looks like she hasn't washed for days. She attempts to be cheerful in spite of everything. She is not the kind of woman who begs. She is holding a small baby, who is asleep. She has the S-27 tag pinned to her dress. JUNE is examining the camera. MAY enters.

MAY: What are you doing?

MAY snatches the camera out of JUNE's hands.

JUNE: I just…

MAY: What?

JUNE: Just having a look.

MAY: Delicate piece of equipment that.

JUNE: Didn't do nothing to it.

MAY: How d'you know?

JUNE: Didn't mean no harm. I just thought, you know, now I'm here, proper, there was things I should know.

MAY: Like?

JUNE: You know. In case /...

MAY: In case of what?

Pause.

JUNE: Just trying to do my job...

MAY: You got em all tagged?

JUNE: All that's out there.

MAY: You mopped the floor?

JUNE: First thing.

MAY: Don't look like it.

JUNE: I did do it.

MAY: You better do it again.

JUNE: Just gets messed up.

MAY: Then do it again. Do you want em to see it like that? Do you?

JUNE: No.

JUNE exits.

MAY checks the camera over.

MOTHER: Hello...

Pause.

Hello...?

MAY repositions the camera on the tripod.

MAY: Name?

MOTHER: Oh gosh, yes, sorry. How rude of me. Hope.

The WOMAN offers MAY her hand. MAY ignores it.

Please do excuse my appearance. Quite dreadful I know. But with things how they are, you know, been wearing the same dress for weeks.

Pause.

And you are?

Pause.

Right. I did ask for some water. Been asking for days but... Well, none to be had... Not for me anyway...

MAY: Sit down.

MOTHER: This used to be a school didn't it?

A bell sounds. The MOTHER jumps.

What was that?

MAY: Lunch.

Pause.

Sit down.

MOTHER: I'd rather stand if you don't mind.

MAY: There ain't nothing to be afraid of.

MOTHER: No?

MAY: No. Ain't gonna hurt you.

MOTHER: Okay.

MAY: Just a photograph.

MOTHER: A photograph?

MAY: Yes.

MOTHER: Oh, no. No. Not in this state. I won't allow it. No. Absolutely not.

MAY: It don't matter.

MOTHER: But people might see.

MAY: They don't care what you look like.

MOTHER: Just give me a second then, would you? A bit of touch up. You understand. Do you have a mirror? A hairbrush?

The baby starts to cry.

Something? You must have something. A pretty girl like you, amongst all these soldiers... A comb? Oh, sssh, sssh, not now, Mummy's busy, not now, sssh, sssh, darling, please. Maybe some lipstick? Anything? Please?

MAY: Ain't got nothing.

MOTHER: Nothing?

MAY: No.

The WOMAN walks over to the window and looks at herself in it.

MOTHER: Don't worry. Only take a moment. That's all. A moment. I promise.

The MOTHER tries to clean her face with spit. The baby's screams are getting louder.

Sssh, sssh, yes, will you please be quiet, please, please.

The baby quietens.

Such a problem child. So demanding. Just screams and screams. Not like my others. Angels the pair of them. They took them away. When we got here. You must have seen them. Faith's adorable, gold curly hair, just like a princess, only seven but so bright for her age, and then there's my little cherub, Earnest, with his pink chubby cheeks, three last week, poor little darling, he must be so scared. You can't miss them. Everyone says it. They're just too sweet.

Pause.

You can't miss them, trust me.

MAY: All look the same after a bit.

MOTHER: Not these two. They're special. Everyone says so.

MAY: When d'you get here?

MOTHER: Three nights ago.

MAY: We did a load of kids, Thursday.

MOTHER: Did you see them?

MAY: Don't remember.

MOTHER: You'd remember.

The WOMAN starts to brush her hair with her fingers.

MAY: We wouldn't keep em long, kids like that.

MOTHER: No?

MAY: No.

Silence.

The baby starts to scream again loudly.

MOTHER: Yes, yes, I know, Mummy's hungry too, I know, I know, quiet, sssh, quiet please…please.

The WOMAN offers the baby to MAY.

27

Here, take him. Please take him. Just for a minute. Just while I arrange myself. I can't do it, I can't do it while he's behaving like this.

MAY takes the baby.

Thank you. You're a life saver. This chair?

MAY: Yes.

The MOTHER sits in the chair. She crosses her legs. The baby has stopped crying.

MOTHER: He likes you.

The MOTHER plumps up her hair.

Which side is better?

The MOTHER shows both profiles.

MAY: Has to be full face.

The MOTHER turns face on. She arranges her hands.

Ready?

MOTHER: Yes.

MAY offers the baby back to the MOTHER.

What are you doing?

MAY: What?

MOTHER: That isn't my baby.

MAY: Yes it is.

MOTHER: No it isn't.

MAY: You came with it.

MOTHER: No, I didn't.

MAY: Yes, you did.

MOTHER: Don't be ridiculous.

MAY: Take it back.

MOTHER: It's not my baby.

MAY: For fuck's sake.

MOTHER: I don't have any children. Do I look like the kind of woman who has children?

MAY: Then who the fuck's is he?

MOTHER: How can you ask that?

MAY: What?

MOTHER: Ask that about your own child.

MAY: Fuck off.

MOTHER: How can you deny him? Your own son? Look at him. He's gorgeous. Who wouldn't want such a gorgeous baby?

MAY: This ain't no joke. D'you see me? I ain't laughing. Take him back. Now. Right now.

MOTHER: He's not mine.

MAY: I don't give a shit.

MOTHER: He's yours.

MAY: I ain't gonna have this.

MOTHER: I know things must be hard at the moment. What with food shortages and two mouths to feed. But don't abandon him like this. I'm begging you. You'll regret it. Regret it for the rest of your life.

MAY: If you don't take him back, I'll have to dispose of him. Right here. Right now. In front of you.

MOTHER: You wouldn't do that. Your own child?

MAY holds the baby upside-down by his feet.

MAY: Ready?

She lifts him up as high as she can, preparing to drop him.

MAY: One… Two…

MOTHER: Stop. Please. He's mine, he's mine.

MAY: Take him.

The MOTHER doesn't move.

MOTHER: You take him please. He's no trouble. Please. I want you to have him. They'd never know.

The baby is gurgling happily in MAY's arms.

He really likes you. I can tell. He'd be really happy with you. You'd be happy together.

Silence.

You know what they'll do to him, if you don't take him, you know what they'll do.

Pause.

MAY dumps the baby in the MOTHER's arms.

MAY: I can't.

Blackout.

SCENE FOUR

The same. The teacher's desk has been removed. There are more racks of tags on the bookcase. A GIRL, several years younger than MAY, sits on the chair. Her uniform is identical to MAY's, but it is dirty and rumpled. Her feet are bare and her face is filthy. The S-27 tag is pinned to her uniform. MAY is taking her picture.

GIRL: Will it hurt?

MAY: What?

GIRL: When they do it?

MAY: Do what?

GIRL: The thing…

MAY: I don't know

Silence.

GIRL: How do they…?

MAY: What?

GIRL: I was just wondering. Maybe it's better, you know, to know. How it's coming. Or maybe it ain't. I dunno.

MAY: Ain't possible, is it? To know. Ain't no-one can tell you.

Pause.

You all right?

GIRL: Don't I look it?

MAY: You look fine.

GIRL: Good.

MAY: Don't see that much.

GIRL: No?

MAY: You're a brave girl.

GIRL: Gotta be brave, in'it? For the Organisation.

MAY: Most people ain't. Shame.

GIRL: What?

MAY: You don't seem nothing like one.

GIRL: I am one.

MAY: How do you know?

GIRL: They told me. It's my own fault, in'it? Ain't nobody else's. I let it get in me. I tried to think if there was somebody. What done it. They kept asking me, over and over again, in my assessment. 'Who was it?' they'd say, 'Who was it what turned you? Give us the names. Or we'll shock you.' But I couldn't think of none. Like no-one what said nothing or done nothing. Must have just caught it. Like a cold.

MAY: Caught it?

GIRL: Like got infected.

MAY: Didn't you feel nothing?

GIRL: Not so's you'd notice.

MAY: No symptoms?

GIRL: You don't know it, like they told us, don't know it till it's too late. You gotta be on your guard. Else the enemy'll get in, like a maggot, then eat its way out from inside.

MAY: You never noticed nothing?

GIRL: Sometimes, when I was out on a run, I'd come out of the shadows and stop for a second, feel the sun on my skin.

MAY: So?

GIRL: You ever been a courier?

MAY: When I was your age. Loved it. Running and running.

GIRL: Stopping, 'gainst the rules, in'it.

MAY: Everyone does it…

GIRL: Ain't all I did. The other day, I'm running. It's hot and it's dusty. Sweat's stuck the dirt to my skin. I come out of the trees, and suddenly there's this big, big lake in front of me. Like the end of the world. The water's bright in the sunshine. Cool. 'Ain't no harm,' it says. So I chuck off my stuff and jump right in. And it's so good, like floating in heaven and I don't never wanna get out. Then the sun starts to dip into the water and the light's going and I get scared and swim back. But my bag and my clothes, they ain't there, where I left em. The water's got em and taken em right out. I jump right back in, the current's all against me, but I fight it and I get em. But when I open the bag, the water... the water's in everything and the words of the message, they been washed right away.

MAY: What d'ya do?

GIRL: Ain't nothing to do. I got to the unit. They saw the blank paper. Arrested. Put on a truck. Brought here.

MAY: Don't seem like much.

GIRL: Sabotage, in'it? Didn't know I was doing that. But I was. Evidence was clear.

Silence.

What do you think happens next? After?

MAY: Ain't thought much about it.

GIRL: My gran used to say that you got born again, but if you were bad it was as a worm or a cockroach or something worse.

MAY: That's what they used to say.

GIRL: Do you think it'd matter? The people you killed?

MAY: What if you ain't got no choice?

GIRL: But if it was like a friend?

MAY: Or family?

GIRL: When they got me, I was only six. I was out playing with Glen. They handed him the bag first. Said they'd shoot the both of us, if he didn't. But he couldn't. He just stood there and peed himself. So I grabbed the bag off him. Put it over his head. Didn't stop to think. Just did it.

MAY: We all did it. Just how they choose, in'it?

GIRL: Gotta save your own skin.

MAY: Couldn't damn you for that.

Silence.

MAY: You don't think they…

GIRL: What?

MAY: They could've made some…

GIRL: Mistake?

MAY: About you?

GIRL: The Organisation?

Silence.

No. Don't never make none do they?

Blackout.

SCENE FIVE

The same. The posters have been removed. There are more racks on the bookcase. They fill the shelves. MAY is changing the film. The entrance door flies open. JUNE shoves a WOMAN through. The WOMAN clings to the door frame resisting her. The WOMAN's clothes are in tatters and the skin hangs loose off her face. She is bruised from head to toe. The S-27 tag is pinned to her. She is terrified.

COUSIN: No. / No. Please. Don't. Please. Please.

JUNE: Get in there.

COUSIN: Help me! / Help me!

JUNE: Get in.

COUSIN: Someone. Please. Please.

JUNE manages to shove the WOMAN through. She slams the door. The WOMAN collapses. She sobs.

Please don't. Please. Please.

MAY: Sit down.

The WOMAN looks up. She calms. MAY takes her notebook.

MAY: Name?

COUSIN: May? May is that you? It is in'it? Thank God. Thank God.

MAY writes down the WOMAN's name in the notebook.

It's me, Lee. Auntie Mead's daughter. Remember? The chubby one. Fat face. That's what you and Brook used to call me. Remember? Ain't so fat now. We thought you was dead. When we found Skye, all shot up like that, we thought ain't gonna be long before we find you and Brook. Where's Brook? She here too? Stupid girl. Taking you in there. We told her, we told her so many times, forest ain't safe. Never listened. Thought she knew better. Stupid, stupid girl. Where is she? Did they do something to her? May? May? Talk to me. Please. I know it's you. You gotta help me. You gotta get me out of this place. They made a mistake. I ain't done nothing. Just took some berries. Off a bush. Ain't nothing. 'Private enterprise,' they said, 'Sabotage.' I don't know what that means. They ask me these questions and I can't answer them, can't answer them right. I was just hungry, May, so hungry. They work us so hard on them farms. Much harder than the old days. May? Please you gotta tell em. They made a mistake. You know me. I ain't no enemy. They can't do this. Not to me. You gotta tell em. / Please...

MAY: Sit still.

COUSIN: May?

MAY: I can't take it.

COUSIN: Oh. Okay.

MAY takes the picture.

MAY: That door.

COUSIN: Yes.

MAY: You leave through that door.

35

COUSIN: And you'll talk to em?

The WOMAN approaches MAY.

You're my only chance, May. You can't let me... Tell em I'm yer cousin. You know what they'll do to me. You can't let em...

The WOMAN touches MAY. MAY instantly recoils.

Remember, remember how I used to get you ice-cream when we went up to town?

The WOMAN grabs hold of MAY.

I know what it is, I know what it is on the other side of that door. You could just open a window. Give me a chance. They'd never know. I can run. Your cousin. May. Your own cousin. Please, please.

The WOMAN starts to shake MAY.

Stop pretending, stop pretending, you don't know me, I know, I know / it's you

MAY: June.

COUSIN: look at me, at me, in my eyes, say you don't / know me

MAY: June!

COUSIN: talk to me, just open your fucking / mouth. You're my

MAY: June!

COUSIN: only hope.

JUNE enters.

May. Please. Will you just fucking

JUNE puts a plastic bag over the woman's head.

God... Stop... May... God...please...please

The WOMAN relaxes her hold on MAY. She sinks down. She clutches at the bag. She dies.

MAY: Thanks.

JUNE: Do the next one yourself.

MAY: She was my cousin.

JUNE: There is no family.

MAY: Don't you think I know?

JUNE: You've gone soft.

MAY: No I ain't.

JUNE: Right.

MAY: I ain't.

JUNE: I'm sick of it, sick of doing your dirty work.

MAY: I shot my own sister.

JUNE: And when was that?

MAY: I still did it.

JUNE: To save your own skin.

MAY: Take her out.

JUNE: It ain't my job.

MAY: Now.

JUNE: It ain't. You're supposed to be training me. Don't even let me touch the camera. All I do is bag and tag, remove the rubbish, bag and tag, all the fucking day.

MAY: Clean. I want it clean in here. Spotless. Before I get back. Understand.

MAY exits.

JUNE: Fuck you. I ain't your fucking slave.

Blackout.

SCENE SIX

The same. The blackboard has been removed and the chair placed on the raised area. The bookshelf is now overflowing with racks of tags. A YOUNG MAN is sitting in the chair. He wears a uniform. He has been severely beaten and his face is badly swollen. The S-27 tag is pinned to him. JUNE is sitting on his lap, smoking. She holds one of his arms pulled taut towards her.

JUNE: Treasonous little shit.

She burns his arm with the cigarette. He winces.

Enjoy it, don't you?

She burns him. He winces.

Like you enjoyed her? Did you? Answer me. Cat ate your tongue? Fucking answer me!

She burns him. He doesn't react. She burns him again. No reaction. She stubs the cigarette out on his arm.

Worth it? Was it? Fucking that cockroach? Opened her legs wide for you, didn't she? Was she dripping for you? Did she beg like a dog for your hard hard cock?

He turns away from her. She grabs his head.

Ah, don't go all shy

MAY enters. She stops.

on me. You ain't fucking shy/ is...

MAY: June.

JUNE: What?

MAY: Enough.

JUNE: Is it?

MAY: Have you seen how many's out there?

JUNE: Yeah.

MAY: Don't you think we should be getting on with it?

JUNE: Do you know what he did?

MAY: I don't care. Get out. Get out now.

> *Pause.*

> Do you want me to get them in here?

JUNE: Fine.

> *JUNE exits, slamming the door behind her. An unbearable silence.*

MAY: Name?

> *Pause.*

> Name?

COL: Ain't got one.

MAY: Yes you have.

COL: I ain't.

MAY: Everyone has.

COL: Not me.

MAY: That ain't true.

> *She writes in the notebook. Silence.*

COL: Ain't you gonna take my picture?

MAY: That's what you want?

COL: Yes.

> *MAY prepares to take the picture. Her finger hovers over the button*
> .

MAY: You don't wanna talk?

COL: Why'd I wanna do that?

MAY: Lots of people do.

COL: Do they?

MAY: Yes.

COL: Best get it over and done with.

MAY: There ain't nothing you need to say?

COL: No.

MAY: No-one you wanna say nothing to?

COL: No.

MAY: No-one?

COL (*Losing his temper.*) Just fucking get on with it, would you?

MAY pushes the button.

We done?

MAY: All done.

COL: That door?

MAY: Yes.

Pause.

COL gets up. MAY moves between him and the exit door.

Don't... I...

COL: What?

Pause.

MAY: Col... ?

COL goes to exit.

Col.

COL: That ain't my name.

MAY: Used to be.

COL: You got the wrong person.

MAY: I know it's you.

COL: You made a mistake.

MAY: No, I ain't.

COL: Get out of my way.

MAY: Col.

COL: Don't.

He goes to exit. MAY blocks his way.

MAY: Stop. Stop right there. I'm ordering you.

COL: Don't do this.

MAY: I can't…

COL: Get out, get out of my fucking way May.

She breaks down. Pause.

Get a grip on yourself.

MAY sobs.

Pull yourself together. Now. What if somebody comes in?

MAY: I don't care.

COL: You're being stupid.

MAY: I won't let you go.

COL: Don't be an idiot. Look at you. You done well. You gonna throw it all away? Just gotta keep going. Ain't gonna be like this for always.

MAY: Ain't it?

COL: Things'll get better.

MAY: When?

COL: They will. Just gotta hold on. Promise.

MAY: Okay.

She reaches out to touch his face. He avoids her.

What did they do to you?

COL: Don't matter. I deserved it.

MAY: I hoped… I… I didn't think I'd see you again. After you left I… I went to them. Said I wanted to go to the front too. Begged em. They wouldn't let me. Said I had to go to college. Learn all this.

COL: You were lucky.

MAY: I watched them trucks roll off along the road, stood there, the sun in my eyes till they weren't nothing, not even a bit of dust. Then I cried. Couldn't stop myself. Ran away and hid.

COL: Always were too soft.

MAY: I missed you.

COL: Weren't nothing, weren't nothing but silly games.

MAY: Not to me.

COL: We were just kids.

MAY: Do you remember that time, I was on a run one way, you on the other. And we crash right into each other in that clearing with that big old tree.

COL: I remember…

MAY: And suddenly, it was like the enemy was all around us.

COL: No way out.

MAY: And I'm shitting myself but you grab me and push me inside the tree. And we're squeezed in there, in the shadows. And I'm shaking, cos the footsteps are getting closer. Suddenly you grip my hand and it's like this shot of heat blasts through me. I can feel your chest pressing into my back. Your heart beating fast. Your breath on my neck.

COL: I remember.

MAY: Then I hear em leaving. Everything's getting quieter and quieter but inside I'm shouting, 'Come back, come back, no, no, no.' Cos I want to stay. Your hand in mine. There, with you.

She touches his hand. He pulls away.

COL: I have to go.

MAY: Stay.

COL: Can't. Ain't possible.

MAY: Ain't it?

She attempts to take his hand again. He evades her.

COL: Don't. Stop it.

MAY: Just for a minute.

COL: Ain't fair. Ain't fair to do this to me. Not now.

MAY: Ain't fair. To get you back. To lose you.

COL: I've gotta go.

MAY blocks his way.

MAY: No.

COL: I ain't him. May. That boy. Not no more. I done terrible things.

MAY: We all have.

COL: Not like me.

43

MAY: I shot my own sister.

COL: That weren't your fault.

MAY: Weren't no-one else's.

COL: Brook had the gun.

MAY: I took it.

COL: Weren't your fault if Brook couldn't choose.

MAY: Between Skye and me?

COL: If you hadn't chosen for her, they would have shot you all. You killed one sister, saved two.

MAY: Saved myself.

COL: No blame in that.

MAY: Ain't there?

COL: Didn't have no choice.

MAY: Did you?

COL: It ain't the same.

MAY: We all done bad things.

COL: Not like me.

MAY: Tell me.

COL: No.

MAY: Used to tell me everything.

COL: Things ain't what they were.

MAY: You ain't changed.

COL: I ain't the same.

MAY: You ain't that different.

COL: Ain't I? D'you know where I been? D'you know where I been all this time? D'you?

MAY: No.

COL: Here.

MAY: Here?

Pause.

Did you know I was…?

COL: Yeah.

MAY: But you didn't…

COL: No.

Silence.

MAY: Where?

COL: Guard. Women's block. You should see em May, you should see em when they come in. Some of them women. They ain't like village women, not some of em, they're different…look you right in the eye…like women on posters…fuck, they make you just wanna touch em, run your fingers all over em, into every nook and cranny, till you ache.

MAY: So?

COL: So the other day they bring this woman to our cell. And she's beautiful. All hips and waist and big brown eyes. Quiet, she is, dead quiet, not weeping or wailing like the others. When they came for em, I'd hide her at the back like she was new and she'd smile at me, just for a second… like thank you. Then night before last, I'm on duty on my own and I can feel her eyes watching me…watching me from her corner. I put out the lamp. Go over. Kiss her. She lets me. Kisses me back. Puts her tongue in my mouth. Lets me touch her. Everywhere. But then when I get there, when I get right inside her, she stops. Dead. Doesn't move a muscle. Rigid, like stone. I pull out. Leave her. Go back to my post. In the dark I can hear her crying…biting down on her fist…whimpering…whining…wheezing like a stuck pig…

Pause.

So… I took a stick… and I… I beat her… beat her… till there weren't no sound any more.

Silence.

Ain't you gonna say nothing?

MAY: Ain't nothing to say.

MAY moves away from him.

COL: May?

He reaches out to touch her.

MAY: Don't.

She recoils from him.

COL: You're angry with me.

Pause.

Ain't what it seems. Just got so lonely. I thought she…that I…

MAY: What?

COL: That if things weren't like this then…but that ain't real… just dreamer's feelings…

Pause.

I thought we could have been…she didn't…

MAY: No.

COL: She just wanted to live.

MAY goes to the camera and winds it on.

MAY: That door.

COL: Look at me.

MAY: That door. Over there.

COL: Not…not like this.

> *Pause.*

> May, look at me. Please. I'm still the same old Col. Honest. Look at me, May, will you look at me.

> *He grabs hold of her.*

MAY: Don't…

> *She struggles.*

> *He turns her towards him.*

> Get the fuck off me.

COL: Look at me.

> *He grabs hold of her head and turns it towards him.*

MAY: Ow. Stop it.

COL: Just fucking look at me, please.

> *MAY closes her eyes.*

> Open your eyes. Open them.

> *He presses MAY against the wall with his body. He attempts to prize open her eyelids with his fingers.*

> Fucking open them.

MAY: June. Help. Help. June!

> *He covers her mouth.*

COL: Don't be stupid.

> *MAY fights back. They struggle.*

MAY: Ow! Ow!

COL: Quiet...for fuck's sake.

MAY: Ow! You're hurting me.

COL: Shut up.

He overpowers her.

MAY: What? You gonna force me are you? You gonna force me like you did her?

Pause.

He kisses her. He continues to kiss her.

A beat.

She kisses him back. They clutch at each other. He finds his way through her clothes. They have sex. It is clumsy and desperate. During it she cries out. They finish.

Silence.

The door opens. They spring apart. JUNE enters.

JUNE: You...?

MAY: Where were you...when I...where the fuck were you?

JUNE: I was busy.

MAY: Doing what?

JUNE: My job. D'you want me to... ?

MAY: No. All under control now.

JUNE: You sure?

MAY: We're nearly done.

JUNE: Have you seen how many's out there? I ain't missing lunch. That door.

MAY: No...not yet. I ain't taken it yet.

JUNE: No?

MAY: No.

JUNE: Go on then.

MAY: In a minute.

JUNE: I could take it.

MAY: No.

JUNE: You could show me.

MAY: No.

JUNE: Do it then.

MAY: Shouldn't you be getting back?

JUNE: What?

MAY: Outside.

JUNE: They're fine.

The sound of a bell.

MAY: You'd better go.

JUNE: I'll go in a minute.

MAY: You wouldn't want to miss it.

JUNE: We'll go together.

MAY: I ain't hungry…you go…bring us something back…

JUNE: Sure?

MAY: Yes.

JUNE: I won't be long.

MAY: Don't be.

JUNE: I won't.

JUNE exits.

MAY: Fuck.

Silence.

We could run.

COL: What?

MAY: Like we used to.

COL: Run?

MAY: Out them windows.

COL: We'd never make it.

Pause.

We could run.

MAY: Yes.

COL: We could run.

Fade.

SCENE SEVEN

The same. There are bars on the windows, which throw long shadows across the room. The room is in chaos. The bookcase is overturned. Round the edges of the room are clumsy piles of racks and tags, all mixed with other rubbish. All sense of order has been destroyed. Only the chair remains in its place. The tripod lies mixed in with the clutter at the side of the room. The camera is on the floor in the centre of the room. The room is filthy. MAY surveys the room. She is wearing normal clothes. She is battered and bruised. She walks over to the camera and picks it up. She examines it. JUNE enters. She stops.

Silence.

JUNE takes the camera out of MAY's hands.

JUNE: Where's your tag?

Pause.

For fuck's sake...

JUNE fishes a tag out of the rubbish and throws it at MAY. Pause.

Ain't you gonna put it on?

MAY pins the tag on. It is the S-27 tag.

Name?

Pause.

Name?

MAY: You know it.

JUNE: I wanna hear you say it.

MAY: May.

JUNE: Spell it.

MAY: M... A... Y...

    JUNE writes slowly.

    Pause.

JUNE: Sit down.

    MAY sits down.

    Comfy?

    Pause.

    Stand up.

    MAY stands up.

    Sit down.

    MAY sits down.

    Stand up.

    MAY stands up.

    Sit down.

MAY sits down.

Stand up.

MAY doesn't.

Stand up!

MAY doesn't.

Do you want me to get them in here?

MAY stands up. Pause.

Sit down.

MAY sits down slowly.

MAY: Just take it please.

JUNE: Smile.

JUNE presses the button. The camera jams. She presses it again. The camera is still jammed.

Fuck.

MAY: What's wrong?

JUNE: Nothing.

JUNE tinkers with the camera. She opens the back to have a look inside.

MAY: You ain't got a clue, have you?

JUNE: I know exactly what I'm doing.

MAY: Send you to college, did they?

JUNE: No. I got talent. I don't need no diploma. Not like you.

JUNE closes the back of the camera and prepares to take MAY's picture.

MAY: What's that button called?

JUNE: What?

MAY: One you got your finger on.

JUNE: What's it matter?

MAY: What's your shutter speed? What aperture you using? What's your depth of field?

JUNE presses the button as if she is taking a picture but the camera is still jammed.

JUNE: That door.

MAY: D'you get it?

JUNE: What?

MAY: The picture. D'you get it?

JUNE: Had yer fella in here the other day. They fucked him up big style. You wanna see?

Pause.

Do you?

Pause.

That door.

MAY gets up to go. She stops.

Scared, are you? Ah…! You always were soft. Thought you could outsmart em. I knew they'd get you. Could've told you. If you'd asked.

MAY: June.

JUNE: Ain't nothing I can do for you now.

MAY: Shutter's still jammed in'it?

JUNE: What?

MAY: It ain't working. The camera. Is it? You couldn't take it.

JUNE: It's fine.

Pause.

MAY: I can fix it.

JUNE: Why'd you wanna do that?

MAY: I can fix it for you.

JUNE: Ain't gonna change nothing.

MAY: I know.

Pause.

JUNE hands over the camera. MAY removes the film.

JUNE: What the fuck are you doing?

MAY: When you opened the back you got light on the film. You lost all the images. Look if you don't believe me.

MAY fixes the camera. JUNE holds the film up and examines it.

JUNE: Fuck.

MAY: You gotta new one?

JUNE: Here.

JUNE fishes a new film out of the pile of clutter and throws it to MAY.

Ain't my fault if I don't know, is it? Ain't my fault if you didn't fucking teach me?

MAY: Thought it'd be better if only I knew.

JUNE: Yeah, keep the best job all to yourself.

MAY finishes fixing the camera and inserting the new film.

MAY: Where's the tripod?

JUNE: Over there, in that corner.

MAY goes to retrieve it.

MAY: What d'you do that for?

MAY untangles the tripod.

JUNE: Was fucking awkward. Thought I'd be like them foreign photographers, used to come down to the front. Take pictures of us kids with our guns. D'you remember?

MAY: Weren't there.

JUNE: They would…like…move around. To get the best shot.

MAY: Can't do it, not in this light. Too dim. Ain't they coming out blurred? The pictures, when you print em?

JUNE: Ain't been printing em. Don't know how, do I? I just been handing the films straight over.

MAY: Fuck.

JUNE: What?

MAY carries the tripod over to the chair.

MAY: You gotta make sure you get enough light on the film, or the image'll be too dark.

She takes three paces to measure roughly three metres. She sets up the tripod there.

You can't use a large aperture, cos then the depth of field's too shallow and the background looks blurred. You gotta slow down the shutter speed, but that means you can't hold it. Cos even if you think you held the camera still, it ain't possible, not for such a long time. You shake, you see? You don't notice it but you do. The whole image gets blurred. And they have to be clear. The images. Or it'll be someone else taking the pictures and you in that chair.

MAY fits the camera onto the tripod.

On the tripod, it's steady. The image is sharp.

JUNE: How the fuck am I supposed to do all that?

MAY: I'm gonna set it up for you. You got a pen?

JUNE: Somewhere.

JUNE finds the pen.

Here.

JUNE throws MAY the pen. MAY marks the position of the tripod on the floor.

MAY: Mark where the feet of the chair are. On the floor.

MAY throws the pen back to JUNE. JUNE marks the position.

Sit in the chair.

JUNE: You're fucking joking.

MAY: No.

JUNE: I ain't sitting there.

MAY: I need someone to focus on.

JUNE: Fucking dead people sat there.

MAY: Don't be stupid.

JUNE sits in the chair. MAY unpins her tag.

Here.

MAY throws the tag to JUNE.

JUNE: What?

MAY: Pin it on.

Pause.

It's for the composition.

Pause.

JUNE: I ain't scared...

MAY: Never said you were.

JUNE pins it on.

JUNE: Hurry up.

MAY adjusts the camera. Her finger hovers over the button.

Don't you push that button. Don't you fucking touch it.

Silence.

MAY finishes with the camera. She stands back.

MAY: There.

JUNE leaps out of the chair. She takes the tag off and hands it back to MAY.

JUNE: Thanks.

MAY takes the tag.

MAY: Better do me again.

She pins on the tag and sits back down in the chair. JUNE looks the camera over suspiciously.

Don't change nothing.

JUNE: How do I know, you ain't just fucked it all up? Set me up for sabotage.

JUNE touches the dial.

MAY: Don't.

JUNE pulls her hand away.

Press the button, that's all you gotta do.

JUNE looks through the lens. Presses the button.

JUNE: There.

MAY gets up.

MAY: Learn where them dials are. Make sure the chair and tripod are on them marks.

JUNE: Right.

MAY: And tidy up. You'll be in shit, if they see mess like this.

JUNE: They don't never come down here.

MAY: They might.

JUNE: Got no reason to.

Pause.

What about them pictures? Them others I took.

MAY: How many?

JUNE: Dunno. Loads. Been doing it ever since you been gone.

MAY: Ain't you been using the tags?

JUNE: Sort of. Not like you did. It ain't possible. Every fucking day there's more and more.

MAY: No-one's said nothing?

JUNE: No.

MAY: Maybe there's too many.

JUNE: Maybe they ain't blurred.

MAY: Maybe they ain't got time to look at em.

JUNE: Maybe no-one ain't never looked at em.

Silence.

MAY: Maybe you're safe.

MAY goes to exit.

JUNE: Stay a bit. If you want.

MAY: It's okay.

JUNE: You ain't afraid are you? Not at all.

MAY: A little. Afraid of not knowing. What comes next. Not of them. I ain't afraid of them no more.

JUNE: Maybe you'll get born better. In one of them rich countries where everyone's got fancy cars and refrigerators.

MAY: Ain't right for some people to have everything and others to have none.

JUNE: You don't believe that?

MAY: Weren't hard to believe. Not where I come from.

JUNE: Never knew I was poor. Not till they came. Thought everyone lived like that. Then one morning, all these trucks full of soldiers come roaring into the village. And leading them, there's this big shiny black car. Music ringing out of it. I ain't never seen nothing like it. It stops in the middle of the village, right in the dirt and a soldier jumps out of one of the trucks, runs over, opens the door. He keeps his eyes to the ground. Out gets this big old man. Dressed like us, just like us, cept his clothes ain't dirty or torn. Don't look like they never saw a field. And when he speaks everyone listens and what he says they does straight away. And no-one dare look at him. Cept me. I can't stop looking, not even if I want to. My eyes are fixed. I see the big fat rings on his fingers, the gold hanging round his neck and his wrists. Then he sees me. Looks straight at me. But I ain't afraid. I look straight back. And he smiles at me, his teeth all golden. And I think I'll have some of that.

MAY: I thought things'd be fairer.

JUNE: Least it's us now, us in charge.

MAY: And that's better?

JUNE: D'you remember the day, when we knew we'd won and we picked up our guns and marched into the city?

MAY: Weren't there.

JUNE: Ah, you missed it. You missed something. We march in and they're cheering us, all them city people in their fancy clothes, cheering us and throwing flowers cos they think the war is over now and they can get back to their lives like they was before, in peace. You should have seen their faces, May, you should have seen em. When the

59

big soldiers turned on em and rounded em up. Made em march, right out of the city, straight off to the farms. No time to pack or nothing. You should have seen their faces.

MAY: Seen too many faces.

JUNE: They was so confused. 'But my house? My car? My money? My shoes?' Like they was leaving their baby or something. And when they was gone, when there weren't nothing left in the city, nothing but dust, us kids, we run round, in and out, everywhere. Into their houses, their gardens, their shops. And there's all this stuff. You should have seen it. The stuff they had. Television sets and typewriters. Jewellery and washing machines. Rooms and rooms of books. We had a right laugh. Chucking stuff out of windows. Making great piles of it, mountains in the street. Driving cars into each other. Setting fire to shit. And everywhere, everywhere, there's this money, this money blowing on the wind, falling like rain, more than I ever seen in my whole life and I'm dancing, May, I'm dancing in it.

Silence.

MAY: Everyone's equal.

JUNE: There's always someone on top, someone at the bottom.

MAY: You don't believe none of it?

JUNE: Never did. Do what you have to. I ain't stupid, stuffed my pockets full of gold, I did. You wouldn't tell them, would you?

MAY: No, I keep my mouth shut.

JUNE: Shame.

MAY: What?

JUNE: Could've been friends.

MAY: Us two?

JUNE: We ain't so different. We could have been mates.

Pause.

You was gone a long time. Thought maybe you made it.

MAY: Nearly did.

JUNE: They always get you. Better to stick it out.

MAY: Is it?

JUNE: I didn't dob you in.

MAY: You didn't?

JUNE: No. I didn't tell em what I saw. So you didn't have to…

MAY: Yes I did. He just walked in the room and it was like the light got turned on again and I didn't want it to go out… My heart pulled my head. Didn't have no choice.

JUNE: Just him. He did that.

MAY: I'd missed him a long time.

JUNE: Should've emptied your heart.

MAY: When we were out there, it was different. Every second. You can't know. The world was on fire. Like I'd been stuck down this well for so long, in the blackness. Just this tiny speck of light way off at the top. And I was reaching and reaching for it but the sides were too slippery, and the light would get further and further away. And all the time, I daren't look below, never, cos of the darkness I knew was under me, case I lost my grip and tumbled right down. Then he came. And we ran. And suddenly the walls burst open and everything around me was burning bright. Like a flame. Can't tell you… I saw it all like I ain't never seen it before. And it was beautiful. The leaves were green. The birds sang. The grass was wet after the rain. The smell of it. The smell of it nearly knocked me over. It was so rich, so strong. And when he'd touch me and hold me and love me, under the moon, under its fierce light, it was like time

61

came undone and there was nothing before or after, just us. And now. And happiness.

JUNE: Just sex, in'it? Fucks with your brain.

MAY: You don't know.

JUNE: Don't I?

MAY: It was like I could see clearly and hear clearly and words had their own meaning again. When people said things I believed em. I didn't never have to watch their eyes to see behind their face. I trusted em. Till that last day. When I thought the miracle had happened. And we stood on the top of that last hill and I could see the red crosses on the top of the tents the other side of the border. The sun was rising. And for the first time I thought we would make it. I laughed. I laughed out loud for joy. And we crashed, through the trees and the undergrowth, down the hill, towards it. Then there they was. Come out from nowhere right in front of us. And I knew someone had betrayed us. Someone had turned us in. And everything went dim.

JUNE: Course they did.

MAY: Don't blame em. Did it to save their own skin.

JUNE: Probably.

MAY: Sad to get a glimpse of everything so bright, then have to leave it. Suddenly there was so much I wanted to do.

JUNE: Should've held on. Should've have waited.

MAY: I'd got so cold. In this place. I needed him.

JUNE: Be colder soon.

MAY: Yes.

JUNE: It ain't gonna last forever.

MAY: Ain't nobody left soon. They'll be killing each other.

JUNE: It'll end.

MAY: Yes.

JUNE: Won't be long.

MAY: No.

JUNE: Should've waited. Cos when it ends. May. When it changes. Where will you be?

MAY: Ain't no-one knows.

JUNE: I'll be here, May. I'll be here.

 Blackout.